The Year We Had To Stay At Home

Written and Illustrated by Ashley Lees

Inspired by and dedicated to Gregor

Book layout by Colin Usher

The Year We Had To Stay At Home : Copyright © Ashley Lees 2021

It all started off like any other day,
when a man on Tv, told us to stay.
Stay in your homes, help keep everyone safe,
It might be difficult but you're being so brave.

There's a virus out there, that might make you sick.
So keep washing your hands, wearing masks, that's the trick.

Schools are closed and you'll learn from home,
but your parents will see, how your mind has grown.

No swimming, no soft play, no trips to the zoo,
we will have to come up with some fun stuff to do.
Like games, science, baking cakes,
even indoor dens we're allowed to make.

Outdoors you're allowed to walk, cycle and run,
thank goodness the summer gave us lots of the sun.

No salons, no barbers, no hairdressers either,
you must stay in isolation if you have a fever.
But you will have two choices, to grow out your hair,
or trust mummy with scissors and hope it's not square.

Not seeing your grandparents or friends for a while now,
mummy's even started to grow her own monobrow.

Essential items, you can only buy.
You have many questions and you're wondering why?

The two metre distance is the rule we all know.
The days have started to become so terribly slow.

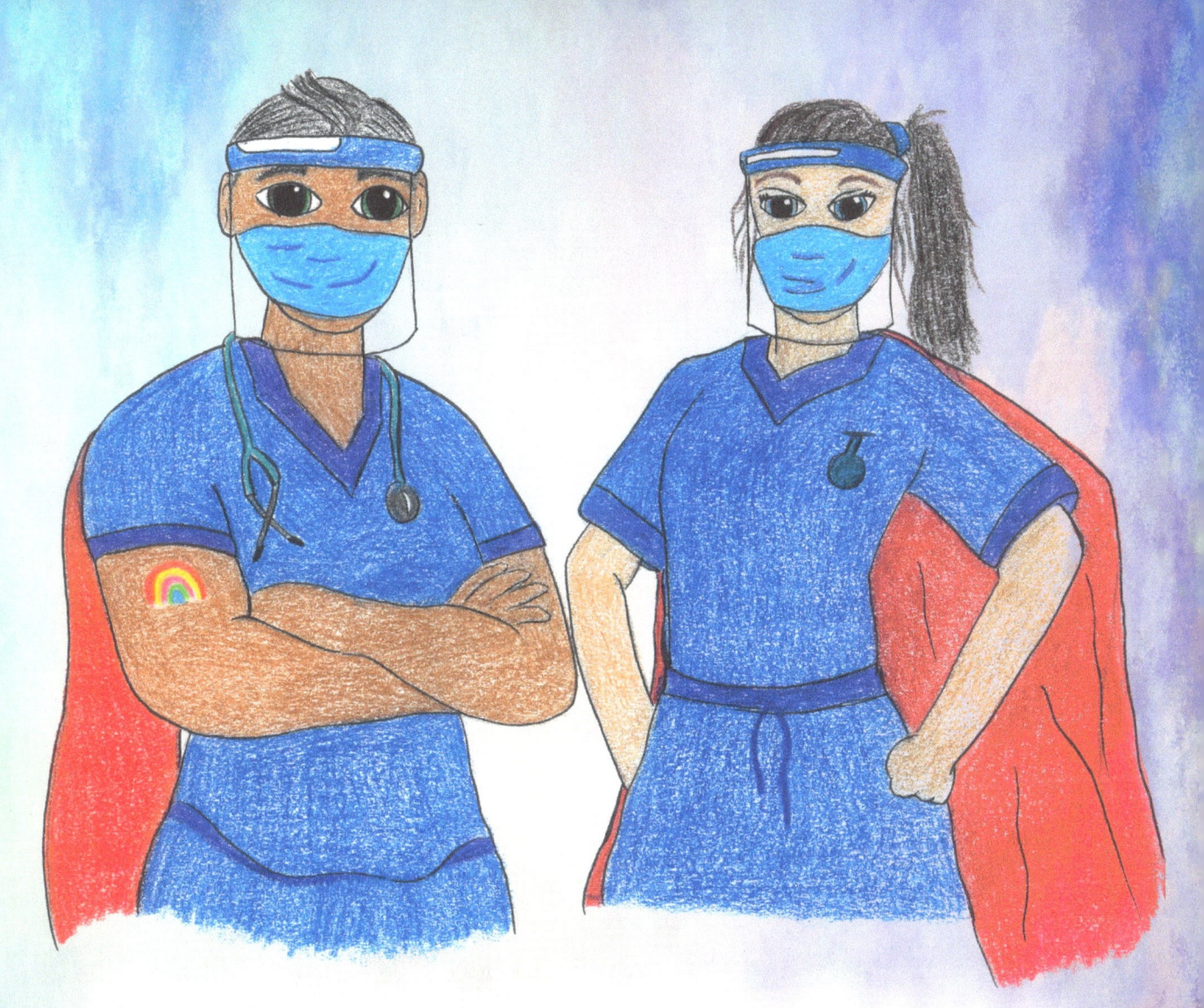

Key workers were heroes through the entire lockdown.
Stay home, stay safe until the numbers drop down,
so we clap and cheer out our windows and doors,
to show our respect, we could hear all of the roars.

It's tough at times and sometimes it's sad,
but think of all the fun we've had.
Times spent together, more than normal, that's for sure.
But they are getting so close to finding a cure.

It's been a difficult year and there's still a long road ahead.
But you've done your best to stop the virus spread.

Just remember you're safe
which is a huge victory
and you've been part of something
that will go down in history.

You Did It!

Activities

Did you spot the hidden rainbows?
How many did you see ? _____

How old were you when
you went into lockdown ?   _____

Who did you spend your lockdown with ? _____

What did you miss the
most whilst in lockdown?   _____ _____

What was your favourite
memory of lockdown?   _____

Did you learn anything
new during lockdown?   _____

Memories
Stick your memories of the lockdown here on these pages

Memories
Stick your memories of the lockdown here on these pages

Memories
Stick your memories of the lockdown here on these pages

Lightning Source UK Ltd.
Milton Keynes UK
UKHW050313221021
392631UK00002B/62